# FROZEN EXTREMES

## JEN GREEN

# Crabtree Publishing Company

www.crabtreebooks.com

# Crabtree Publishing Company

www.crabtreebooks.com

**Author:** Jen Green

**Editor:** Molly Aloian

**Proofreaders:** Adrianna Morganelli, Katherine Berti

**Project coordinator:** Robert Walker

**Production coordinator:** Margaret Amy Salter

**Prepress technician:** Margaret Amy Salter

**Project editor:** Tom Jackson

**Designer:** Lynne Lennon

**Picture researchers:** Sophie Mortimer, Sean Hannaway

**Managing editor:** Tim Harris

**Art director:** Jeni Child

**Design manager:** David Poole

**Editorial director:** Lindsey Lowe

**Children's publisher:** Anne O'Daly

**Photographs:**
Alamy: Andy Sutton: page 13 (right)
Ardea: Chris Knights: page 11 (top); Andrey Zvoznikov: pages 12 (top), 16 (left)
Corbis: George Steinmetz: page 6 (bottom); Stock Photos: page 7 (bottom); David Muench: page 12 (bottom); Thorsten Milse: page 18 (top); Denis Scott: pages 20-21 (top); Wolfgang Kaehler: page 23 (top); Danny Lehman: page 23 (bottom); Bettmann: page 24 (top); Galen Rowell: pages 24 (bottom), 29 (bottom); Underwood & Underwood: page 25
FLPA: Colin Monteath: page 7 (top)
NaturePL: Jane Burton: page 17 (bottom)
Photolibrary Group: Marco Simoni: page 5 (bottom); Enrique Aquirre: pages 8-9; Mark Newman: page 9 (top); Fridmar Damm: pages 10-11; Theo Allofs: page 13 (left); Gerard Soury: pages 14-15; Lon E. Lauber: page 15 (bottom); Andy Whale: page 17 (top); Corbis: pages 18-19, 21 (top); Digital Vision: page 19 (top)
Shutterstock: Armin Rose: pages 4-5, 27 (top); Sarunas Krivickas: page 5 (top); Serg Zastavkin: pages 11 (bottom), 26 (bottom); Keith Levit: page 14 (top); JG Photo: page 15 (top); Halldor Eiriksson: page 16 (right); Vladimir Melnik: page 19 (bottom); Fernando Rodrigues: page 20 (bottom); Christian Musat: page 21 (bottom); Tyler Olson: page 22; Steve Estvanik: page 26 (top); Iakov Kalinin: page 27 (bottom); Dmitry Pichugin: page 28; Pavel Pustina: page 29 (top); Jan Martin Will: front cover

**Illustrations:**
Darren Awuah: page 9

Every effort has been made to trace the owners of copyrighted material.

---

**Library and Archives Canada Cataloguing in Publication**
Green, Jen
    Frozen extremes / Jen Green.

(Extreme nature)
Includes index.
ISBN 978-0-7787-4502-0 (bound).--ISBN 978-0-7787-4519-8 (pbk.)

    1. Ecology--Polar regions--Juvenile literature.  2. Animals--Polar regions--Juvenile literature.  3. Plants--Polar regions--Juvenile literature.  4. Polar regions--Juvenile literature.  I. Title. II. Series: Extreme nature (St. Catharines, Ont.)

QH541.5.P6G73 2008          j577.0911          C2008-907340-1

**Library of Congress Cataloging-in-Publication Data**
Green, Jen.
   Frozen extremes / Jen Green.
     p. cm. -- (Extreme nature)
   Includes index.
   ISBN 978-0-7787-4519-8 (pbk. : alk. paper) -- ISBN 978-0-7787-4502-0 (reinforced library binding : alk. paper)
   1. Cold regions. 2. Cold-blooded animals. I. Title. II. Series.

   GB641.G76 2009
   910.911--dc22
                                                    2008048640

---

## Crabtree Publishing Company

www.crabtreebooks.com          1-800-387-7650

**Published in Canada**
**Crabtree Publishing**
616 Welland Ave.
St. Catharines, Ontario
L2M 5V6

**Published in the United States**
**Crabtree Publishing**
PMB16A
350 Fifth Ave., Suite 3308
New York, NY  10118

# CONTENTS

# INTRODUCTION

Picture a world where snow and ice stretch in all directions. There are no trees, plants, or people. The glare from the low sun is blinding. An icy wind stings your skin, and any exposed areas go numb very quickly. You are in the extreme world of the frozen zones.

▶ *In the frozen polar regions, both land and sea are covered in thick ice for at least part of the year.*

## HOME OF ICE

Ice covers ten percent of Earth's surface. Nearly all of this is in the **polar regions**, in the far north and south. The limits of the polar regions are marked by the Arctic and Antarctic circles.

## ALWAYS COLD

The Arctic and Antarctic are always cold because the sun is never high in the sky. To reach the ground, the sun's rays have farther to travel through more of the air. This weakens the rays' heating power.

## In the Extreme

Far outside the polar regions, mini frozen zones exist on high mountains. They are called glaciers. Glaciers are frozen rivers of ice. They flow very slowly downhill (*left*). As they move, glaciers grind away at rocks and cut valleys through the mountains.

## ICEBERGS

The glaciers in the polar regions flow down toward the coast. When they reach the ocean, they break up to form floating icebergs (*left*). Tall, spiky Arctic icebergs tower up to 300 feet (91 m) high. Antarctic icebergs are mostly flat-topped because they break off the huge floating ice shelves that cover the sea.

## ARCTIC AND ANTARCTIC

The Arctic and Antarctic have similar **climates**, but they are also very different from each other. In the far north, the Arctic is mainly an ice-covered ocean, surrounded by the coasts of North America, Scandinavia, and Russia. The largest Arctic landmass is Greenland—also the world's largest island. At the opposite end of Earth, the Antarctic is covered by a **continent** called Antarctica. Antarctica is twice the size of Australia. The land is covered by an immense sheet of ice—up to 2.5 miles (4 km) thick.

## NORTH AND SOUTH POLES

The North Pole is the most northerly point on the planet. At the North Pole, you are standing on **sea ice** about 6 feet (1.8 m) deep, floating on top of the Arctic Ocean. The South Pole is located high on Antarctica's ice cap near the middle of the icy continent.

▼ *Seen from space, the white masses of Greenland and the Arctic ice seem to change shape throughout the year. In winter they expand, and in summer they shrink again as the sea ice melts.*

### In the Extreme

Antarctica is the windiest place on Earth. Gusts of up to 200 miles per hour (321 km/h) have been recorded here. It is often too windy for planes to land. One explorer called his Antarctic base "Kingdom of the Blizzards."

Greenland

Arctic Ocean ice

## FAST FACTS

⭐ The highest mountain in Antarctica is Vinson Massif (*right*), at 16,800 feet (5,120 m) tall.

⭐ The thickness of the ice makes Antarctica the world's highest continent. At an **average** of 8,000 feet (2,438 m) high, it is three times higher than any other continent.

⭐ Tall mountains stick out of the ice near the coast. However, further inland, the weight of the ice pushes much of the land below sea level. If the ice cap ever melted, the land would spring back up again!

▼ *Paradise Harbor is a tiny base located among the mountains of the Antarctic Peninsula near the tip of South America.*

## LIFE IN THE FREEZER

Arriving in the polar regions by plane is like entering a freezer! Fingers, toes, and noses can be at risk of **frostbite**—even in summer. Hot drinks freeze in seconds when taken outdoors. In the extreme cold your spit would freeze before it hits the ground!

## KEEPING COLD

**Temperatures** in the Arctic rarely rise much above freezing even in summer. In winter, they can fall as low as -40 °F (-40 °C). This is warm compared to Antarctica, which is Earth's coldest place. The average temperature at the South Pole is -56 °F (-49 °C). The coldest temperature ever recorded there was -128 °F (-89 °C).

▼ *People need to be well prepared to visit the polar regions. They need thick, waterproof clothes to protect them from the wind.*

## In the Extreme

The polar regions are really deserts because so little rain falls there. The Arctic receives less than 10 inches (25 cm) of rain or snow annually. Antarctica gets even less—only about 1.9 inches (4.8 cm) per year. That is less than any of the world's hot deserts. Rain is rare because moisture is locked away as solid ice.

КАПИТАН ХЛЕБНИКОВ

QUARK

## DIFFERENT SEASONS

The polar regions have the most extreme seasons. In summer, temperatures rise above freezing for a few days at a time. In fact, there are no nights—the sun never sets in summer. It just dips close to the **horizon**. However, this "warm" season lasts a couple of months before the freezing conditions return. The rest of the time the poles are bitterly cold.

*The clear nights of the Arctic winter and fall are the best time to see the northern lights—a glowing effect in the sky.*

*Arctic winter*

*day*

*axis*

*Arctic circle*

*Antarctic circle*

*Antarctic summer*

*night*

## LANDS OF THE MIDNIGHT SUN

In most places, the sun sets and rises as Earth spins on its **axis** every 24 hours. However, in summer, the sun never sets near the North and South poles. It is light 24 hours a day—even at midnight! In winter, the sun never rises, and it is dark all the time. This is because Earth's axis is tilted. In summer, each pole points toward the sun and is always bathed in sunlight even as the planet turns.

# PLANT LIFE

All plants need sunlight, warmth, and liquid water to thrive. The plants of the frozen zones struggle with long months of darkness, freezing temperatures, and desert-like conditions. Only the very toughest plants can live in this harsh world.

## ON THE TUNDRA

No plants grow at the poles and on the highest mountains because the ground is always covered in ice. The only plants in Antarctica are on the coasts or on islands, where the weather is a bit milder. The land surrounding the Arctic Ocean is covered with bleak, treeless plains. This habitat is called tundra. South of the tundra grows a dark evergreen forest called the taiga.

## In the Extreme

Land plants struggle to survive in the frozen zones, but polar seas are rich in **microscopic** plants called plankton. These miniature floating plants provide food for equally tiny animals. In spring, the plankton grow in number. They cover the water's surface in a blanket of food. Plant and animal plankton form the base of **food chains** in the seas.

## ALWAYS FROZEN

Beneath the topsoil on the tundra, the ground is permanently frozen. This rock-hard ice layer is called permafrost. In summer, the snow melts and the topsoil thaws out, but water cannot drain through the frozen ground. It makes pools on the surface, turning the tundra into huge marshes (*right*).

▼ *Only small plants like mosses can grow in the polar regions.*

## FAST FACTS

★ One of the most northerly trees in North America is the white spruce of the Canadian Arctic.

★ In Siberia, the gmelin larch survives even farther north—hundreds of miles north of the Arctic circle.

★ The most northerly flowering plant is the yellow saxifrage (*left*), with its mini rosettes of tough, waxy leaves.

## PLANTS OF THE TUNDRA

The name *tundra* means "treeless." It is too cold and there is not enough water for tall trees to grow in this bleak, windswept place. Low-growing shrubs and plants stay close to the ground, away from the icy winds. Plant roots cannot penetrate the permafrost, so they spread along the ground, gathering every last drop of moisture.

▲ *Polar plants, such as this polar poppy, are covered in hairs to keep them warm.*

## PLANTS OF THE TUNDRA

Amazingly, about 1,700 different types of plants manage to grow in the Arctic. Nearly one third of these are hardy mosses and **lichens**, but there are also flowering plants, tufts of cotton grass, and heaths covered in bilberry and blueberry bushes.

### In the Extreme

Lichens **survive** farther north than any plant. Lichens are not really plants, but a combination of tiny **algae** and **fungus**. Like plants, the algae produce food using sunlight energy, while the fungus provides shelter and moisture. Reindeer moss is a yellow lichen that looks like little deer antlers. The lichen is a summer food for herds of caribou.

# FAST GROWERS

Tundra plants have to cope with an incredibly short growing season. Winter lasts for at least nine months. Temperatures rise above freezing for just 50 days a year. Plants use the long hours of daylight to grow, flower, and produce seeds. In August, the winter chill returns. Plants and seeds survive the winters under a blanket of snow that protects them from frost.

## FAST FACTS

* Dwarf trees are able to survive harsh conditions ordinary trees cannot tolerate. The Arctic willow (*below*) grows to just three inches (7.6 cm) tall, but spreads along the ground for up to 16 feet (4.8 m). In summer, it produces large flowers to attract insects. The trees grow incredibly slowly and can live for 250 years.

▲ *Bilberries are harvested in Scandinavia to make tasty juices and are eaten over ice cream.*

# ANIMAL LIFE

A surprising number of animals live in the Arctic despite the harsh climate. Many are summer visitors that spend their winters in warmer regions to the south. However, only a few **species** remain in the far north all year round.

*▲ Polar bears live on the Arctic ice. They are also excellent swimmers and can paddle for miles using their wide paws.*

## TOO COLD FOR LIFE

No animals survive far inland in Antarctica —the climate is just too cold. However, the oceans around the continent are packed with fish. Sea birds and seals rest on the coast. The Arctic Ocean also has many fish. They are smaller and swim slower in the cold water than in other oceans. The Arctic ice is home to seals and walruses. Land **mammals**, such as caribous, live on the tundra. In summer, birds arrive to feed on the insects swarming over tundra pools.

## In the Extreme

The Arctic fox's coat changes color with the seasons to provide **camouflage**. The summer coat is brown to blend in with the rocky landscape. The white winter coat (*above*) blends in with the snow. Arctic hares and weasels also change color to match the surroundings.

## KEEPING WARM

Mammals of the frozen zones keep warm with the help of thick fur. Most mammals have a double fur coat. A long, outer coat of thick hairs keeps the snow off. Fine **underfur** keeps the body warm. Arctic animals have smaller ears than their cousins in warmer regions to stop them from getting frostbitten. Sea mammals do not have many hairs. Instead, they stay warm with layers of **blubber**.

◄ *Walruses use their long tusks to haul themselves on to floating ice. Males have the longest tusks.*

## Vital Statistics

★ The musk ox lives on the tundra. It has the longest hairs in the world, which grow three feet (91 cm).

★ These shaggy beasts (*left*) look like bison but are in fact giant sheep.

★ Their hooves are very wide so they act like snowshoes, keeping the ox from sinking into soft snow.

## SUMMER VISITORS

In summer, there is plenty of rich insect food on the tundra and only a few **predators**. That makes it an excellent place to lay eggs and raise chicks. Dozens of species of birds fly thousands of miles to reach it each year. In summer, cliffs and lakes are crowded with nests. In autumn, the birds fly south again. These long annual journeys are called **migrations**.

## FAST FACTS

★ Arctic terns breed on the tundra in May and June. As the Arctic summer ends, they fly all the way to Antarctica, where summer is just beginning.

★ Some terns (*below*) complete a round trip of up to 16,000 miles (25,749 km) in a year.

◀ *A red-breasted goose keeps its chicks warm in a nest in the Russian Arctic.*

## In the Extreme

Most caribou (*right*) spend winter in the sheltered taiga forests, where they eat twigs and bark. In spring, the deer trek hundreds of miles north to give birth on the tundra. The gangly calves can stand and walk just a few minutes after birth. In autumn, the calves follow the herd back to the forest.

## LAB WORK

In many parts of Europe and North America, you can see Arctic geese, swans, and ducks passing by on migration. Birds and mammals in your area prepare for winter by feeding, just as in the Arctic. Bats and ground squirrels hibernate. Make a note of the first date you see these animals in spring, and the last date you see them in autumn.

## ALL YEAR ROUND

Some creatures tough it out in the Arctic all year round, enduring the long months of winter. Voles and lemmings survive in a network of tunnels under the snow. Ground squirrels and polar bears **hibernate** in winter. Arctic foxes stay active, scavenging for scraps of food.

▶ *Voles are kept warm in the Arctic winter by a blanket of snow on the ground.*

## WEB OF LIFE

The plants and animals of the tundra form a web of life. Plants and lichens form the base of the food chain, feeding animals, such as caribou and lemmings. Insects hatch in spring and provide food for nesting birds and chicks. Small predators, such as foxes and weasels, prey on chicks, eggs, and lemmings. In turn, they may be eaten by top predators, such as wolves and polar bears.

## RACE AGAINST TIME

Most animals of the frozen zones raise their young in the very short summer. Food is easy to find, and the long hours of daylight provide plenty of time for hunting. Brant geese rear their young in an incredibly short time. They arrive on the tundra in June, and lay their eggs immediately. The chicks hatch and grow quickly. In under two months, the young birds are ready for the flight south.

## POLAR BEAR CUBS

Polar bear cubs are born in winter, in a den dug in the snow. The mother is hibernating during the birth and sleeps for the next three months as her cubs drink her rich milk. When spring arrives, the mother breaks out of the den, and the cubs go outside for the first time.

# In the Extreme

Emperor penguins are the only animals to spend winter in Antarctica. A female leaves her single egg with her mate and heads to the sea to find food. The males balance their eggs on their feet and huddle together for warmth. They take turns standing in the middle of the group. The chicks hatch after two months, when the females return to take over for the males.

## Vital Statistics

★ Harp seals (*left*) are gray as adults, but their babies are white so they can hide on the ice.

★ The mother feeds her pup for just five days, the shortest time of any mammal. Harp seal milk is 50 percent fat. Cow's milk is just three percent.

▲ *Seals gather on beaches in summer to give birth and then breed. The pregnant mothers spend the winter at sea.*

## OCEAN FOOD CHAINS

As on land, the **marine** plants and animals in polar zones are linked in a web of life. In spring and summer, shrimp-like creatures called krill eat plankton. Krill are pink and are so common that they turn the sea red in places. Krill provide food for fish, squid, and giant whales. In the Antarctic, penguins feed on fish, while penguins themselves are food for leopard seals and killer whales.

## FEEDING UNDER WATER

Giant whales, such as humpbacks and blue whales, sieve krill from great gulps of water. They do this using comb-like baleen plates hanging inside their mouths. Humpback whales also eat fish. They blow bubbles around a group of fish to herd them together before swallowing them all at once.

## Vital Statistics

* Earth's largest living animal, the blue whale, measures up to 100 feet (30 m) long and can weigh 150 tons (135 tonnes).

* Blue Whales breed in warm water and migrate to polar seas in summer to feast on krill.

## NOISY WHALES

Belugas are small, toothed whales from the Arctic. Their white skin camouflages them among the icebergs. These whales live in groups, or pods. They communicate with one another using clicks, squeals, and bell-like clangs. Sailors call them sea canaries.

# KILLER SEAL

The leopard seal is the largest and
fiercest seal in the Antarctic. It preys
on penguins (*below*) by tipping up
the floating ice on which the birds
rest. Then it snaps up its prey with
sharp, pointed teeth. These seals
grow up to 13 feet (4 m) long
and have spotted coats
like leopards.

▲ *Penguins move slowly on
land, but they "fly" quickly
through the water by
flapping their wings.*

# THE HUMAN EXPERIENCE

People have lived in the Arctic for centuries. Arctic groups include the Inuit of North America, the Chukchi of Siberia, and the Saami of Scandinavia. Antarctica is **uninhabited,** unless you count the scientists living on research bases.

## SEAL HUNTERS

The Inuit people are the largest Arctic group. They traditionally hunt seals and whales using harpoons. In summer, they gather berries and eggs, catch fish, and hunt for caribou. The Inuit hunt using skin-covered canoes called kayaks. Their homes are made of turf and stone.

## In the Extreme

The Inuit traditionally camp in shelters called igloos (*below*) on hunting trips. These dome-shaped huts are made of blocks of ice that spiral to the top. An oil-burning lamp makes life comfortable inside even when a howling blizzard is raging outside.

▲ *An Inuit in traditional clothes made from caribou furs stands in front of his tent during a summer hunting trip in the Canadian Arctic.*

## DEER FARMERS
The Saami people of Scandinavia are also sometimes called Lapps. Unlike the Inuit, the Saami are herders, not hunters. The Saami keep huge herds of reindeer. They followed the herds as they moved to the tundra in summer and south to the forests in winter. Reindeer provided meat and milk, and skins to make tents and clothing. Bones and antlers were shaped into tools and weapons.

## HUSKY TEAMS
In the past, Inuit people used sleds pulled by tough dogs called huskies to haul their possessions when they moved camp. Most teams contained 12 dogs hitched either in a fan shape or in a long line of pairs. Today, husky sleds are used mainly for racing.

## SOUTHERNERS ARRIVE

In the 1600s, Europeans came to the Arctic looking for a way through to Asia. There was no easy route, but people returned to hunt whales, seals, and foxes. The southerners also came in search of **minerals**. In the 1880s, the discovery of gold in Alaska started a **gold rush**. In 1909, U.S. navy officer Robert Peary finally reached the North Pole with the help of Inuit guides and huskies.

▼ *People now live at the South Pole all year. One base is inside a giant dome. The dome is slowly sinking into the ice, so another base has been built nearby on stilts.*

✳ **IN 1911**, Norwegian explorer Roald Amundsen became the first person to reach the South Pole (*below*). He beat a British team led by Robert Scott. Amundsen's team used skis and sleds pulled by huskies. The British team hauled their own sleds, and they all died on the way back.

## CHANGING WAYS

The newcomers brought many changes to the Arctic. Few Arctic people now live the traditional life of hunting or herding. Most now wear modern, waterproof clothing and live in houses.

## DISCOVERY OF ANTARCTICA

Antarctica was discovered by seal hunters in the 1820s. By the 1950s, many countries had claimed a slice of the continent, but in 1959, all of them agreed to set aside their claims. They decided Antarctica should be used only for peaceful scientific study. Mining and constructions are not allowed.

## In the Extreme

In 1893, Norwegian explorer Fridtjof Nansen tried to reach the North Pole by ship, drifting in the sea ice. However, the ice carried him too far south. In 1958, the U.S. Navy submarine Nautilus became the first ship to sail to the North Pole—by traveling under the ice!

## GREAT FAILURE

In 1912, Irish explorer Ernest Shackleton set out to cross Antarctica. However, his ship was slowly crushed by the ice (*right*). He and his crew escaped by lifeboat to Elephant Island. From there, Shackleton and five men crossed 800 miles (1,287 km) of stormy ocean. They reached the island of South Georgia to get help and rescue the rest of the crew.

▲ Cruise ships take tourists to the frozen zones. People can take boat trips around huge icebergs and see the northern lights from the comfort of the luxury ship.

## SCIENTISTS ON ANTARCTICA

There are about 80 research bases in Antarctica today, but many are staffed only in summer. Polar scientists have made many exciting discoveries about wildlife and the climate. They now also believe that Antarctica is actually two separate pieces of land.

## TOURISM

Tourism is a new industry in the frozen zones. Antarctica, much of Greenland, and parts of Alaska, Canada, and Siberia are protected in huge wildlife reserves.

## COUNTDOWN

Survival is impossible in the polar regions without warm, waterproof clothing. Your skin would start to freeze in minutes and you would soon die of **hypothermia**. You would also need a stove, saucepan, and matches to melt ice for water, and a knife to cut a shelter in the ice. You would definitely need a flashlight in winter!

*The Arctic ice cap may one day break apart enough for large cargo ships to travel through the Arctic Ocean.*

## GLOBAL WARMING

Scientists think that Earth's climate is getting warmer. The changes to the world's climate appear to be melting the ice in the frozen zones. Sea ice floats, so melting that does not really change the sea level. However, if the huge **freshwater** ice caps on Greenland and Antarctica melted, it would make the world's oceans rise so much that coastal cities would be flooded. The problem is caused by waste gases given off as we burn fuels. The way to fix the problem is to use less of these fuels and switch to cleaner energy sources.

## FAST FACTS

* Most northern capital is Nuuk, Greenland (population 15,000).

* Largest settlement on Antarctica is the U.S. research base at McMurdo Sound. It holds up to 1,250 people.

* In 1967, Antarctica's highest peak, Vinson Massif, was scaled for the first time by U.S. climbers.

* In 1978, Japanese explorer Naomi Uemura became the first person to walk to the North Pole alone.

* In 1993, British explorer Ranulph Fiennes crossed Antarctica on foot.

* Largest city in the Arctic is Murmansk, Russia, a port (below) with a population of 325,000.

# EXTREME FACTS

## ICEBERGS

There are several types of icebergs. Tall, craggy icebergs are called pinnacle bergs. Smaller hunks of ice are called bergy bits. Growlers are named for the noise they make as they melt. Less than one fifth of an iceberg shows above the surface; the rest is under water.

## SPONGY PLANT

Sphagnum moss grows in boggy parts of the tundra. The dense cushion of vegetation soaks up water—you can use it as a sponge.

## ICE AGES

Ice ages are periods in the past when Earth was colder than today. During the last Ice Age, which ended 10,000 years ago, the northern frozen zone covered most of North America, Europe, and Asia.

## SHELVES OF ICE

Huge floating ice sheets surround the edge of Antarctica. The biggest, the Ross Ice Shelf, is the size of France.

## HOT AND COLD

Frozen zones have volcanoes: Kamchatka (*below*) in east Asia is the most volcanic place on land. There are also eruptions on the seabed under the frozen Arctic Ocean.

## OLD AND COLD
Lichens are among Earth's oldest living things. Some Arctic lichens are thought to be 4,000 years old.

## EXTREME ANIMALS
The Arctic fox keeps warm on freezing nights by curling up in the snow and using its long bushy tail like a muff, to keep its nose warm.

## NORTHWEST PASSAGE
For centuries, explorers searched for the Northwest Passage—a sea route to Asia via northern Canada. In 1906, Norwegian explorer Roald Amundsen found a way through the maze of ice and islands.

## HUNTER AND HUNTED
Wolves are one of the top predators of the tundra. These clever pack animals hunt reindeer and musk oxen. The oxen form a circle with their young in the middle. They lower their heads to block the wolves with a wall of horns.

## ICEBREAKERS
Ships called icebreakers (*below*) keep polar shipping lanes free of ice. Their bows are reinforced with steel to crack thick ice.

## ICE TOWN
The coldest town in the world is Verkhoyansk, Siberia, in eastern Russia. In 1892, a temperature of -93 °F (-69 °C) was recorded. However, people still continue to live there, working as fur trappers and reindeer farmers.

# GLOSSARY

**algae** Tiny plant-like animals

**average** A normal amount that is not too small and not too large

**axis** The line running through Earth around which the planet spins

**blubber** Thick fat under the skin

**camouflage** Coloring that blends in with the surroundings

**climate** Weather patterns

**continent** A large mass of land

**food chains** Patterns of eating and being eaten

**freshwater** Water without salt

**frostbite** Damage caused when skin and muscles are frozen

**fungus** A type of living thing that includes mushrooms and molds

**gold rush** When many people travel to an area to look for gold

**hibernate** To sleep through the winter

**horizon** The line between land or water and the sky

**hypothermia** When the body gets too cold to work properly

**lichens** Moss-like growths that cover rocks in cold places.

**mammals** A group of animals that have hairy bodies and feed young with milk

**marine** Related to the oceans

**microscopic** Too small to see without a microscope

**migrations** Journeys made by animals from one place to another each year

**minerals** Natural chemicals

**polar regions** The areas at the top and bottom of Earth

**predators** Hunting animals

**sea ice** Ice made from frozen seawater

**species** A group of animals that are very closely related to each other

**temperatures** A measure of how hot or cold something is

**underfur** Fine fur covering the skin

**uninhabited** When no one lives in a place

# FURTHER RESOURCES

## BOOKS

**Around the Poles** by Robert Snedden. North Mankato, MN: Smart Apple Media, 2005.

**Life on the Ice** by Susan E. Goodman. Minneapolis, MN: Millbrook Press, 2006.

**Polar Regions** by Sally Morgan. Chicago, IL: Raintree, 2004.

**Survivor's Science in the Polar Regions** by Peter D. Riley. Chicago, IL: Raintree, 2005.

**Why Are the North and South Poles So Cold?** by Patricia J. Murphy. New York, NY: PowerKids Press, 2004.


## WEBSITES

**National Geographic Global Warming Quiz**

science.nationalgeographic.com/science/environment/global-warming/quiz-global-warming.html

**National Geographic Virtual Antarctica**

www.nationalgeographic.com/crittercam/antarctica/

**Northern Lights Generator**

www.mrnussbaum.com/aurora/

**U.S. Antarctic Program South Pole Webcam**

www.usap.gov/videoClipsAndMaps/spWebCamAlt.cfm

# INDEX

Printed in the U.S.A. — BG